Manuel Makes a Map!

Karen Klimchuk

Rosen Readers

Rosen Classroom™

New York

Published in 2014 by The Rosen Publishing Group, Inc.
29 East 21st Street, New York, NY 10010

Book Design: Jon D'Rozario

Photo Credits: Cover, pp. 5, 7, 9, 21 (boy) Rob Marmion/Shutterstock.com; pp. 7, 9, 11, 13, 15, 17, 19, 22 (paper) jannoon028/Shutterstock.com; p. 11 Ansis Klucis/Shutterstock.com; p. 13 Africa Studio/Shutterstock.com; p. 15 MilousSK/Shutterstock.com; p. 17 Neo Edmund/Shutterstock.com; p. 19 Khafizov Ivan Harisovich/Shutterstock.com; p. 22 Tang Yan Song/Shutterstock.com.

ISBN: 978-1-4777-2319-7
6-pack ISBN: 978-1-4777-2320-3

Manufactured in the United States of America

CPSIA Compliance Information: Batch #CS13RC: For further information contact Rosen Publishing, New York, New York at 1-800-237-9932.

Contents

Fun with Maps!

Manuel is learning about maps in school. Some maps show the streets in a city, and some maps show all the states in our country. Special maps called **globes** show the whole world! Manuel wants to learn how to make a map by himself. His teacher, Mrs. Harris, shows his class how to make a map of their classroom.

It's fun to look at maps.
You can find places you want to visit!

Letters and Numbers

The kind of map Manuel learns to make is called a grid. It's made up of lots of little squares that he makes with **horizontal** and **vertical** lines. The grid Manuel makes for himself has 16 squares. Across the top of the grid, Manuel writes letters. There are four **columns**, so he writes the first four letters of the alphabet: A, B, C, and D.

The letters on the grid will help Manuel show people where things are in his classroom.

A B C D

Manuel writes a number on the side for each row of the grid. Since there are four squares in the first column, Manuel writes the numbers 1, 2, 3, and 4. Each square is named using a letter and a number. The square on the upper left of the map is called A1.

The upper left square is called A1 because that's where column A and row 1 cross each other. The star is in square D4.

A
B
C
D
1
2
3
4
A1

What's a Key?

The first thing Manuel wants to put on his grid is his desk. His desk is too hard to draw, though. Mrs. Harris tells him he can use a brown rectangle as a **symbol** for his desk. Then, he can draw the symbol in a place called the key. A key tells what the symbols on a map mean.

When Manuel reads his map, he puts the letters and numbers together to say where something is. His desk is in square C2.

A
B
C
D
1
2
3
4
Key
= Manuel's desk

Making a Grid

Manuel wants to put Mrs. Harris's desk on his map, too. This is where she sits when Manuel and his friends are working by themselves. Manuel uses a green rectangle as the symbol for her desk. Mrs. Harris sits in the front corner of the classroom, so he draws her desk in square D1.

Mrs. Harris is a good teacher!
She likes to teach her students how to use maps.

A B C D
1
2
3
4
Key
= Manuel's desk
= Mrs. Harris's desk

Manuel's friend Gabriella sits next to him in class. He wants to put her desk on his grid, but he doesn't want to use another brown rectangle. That would look the same as his desk. He uses a purple rectangle for Gabriella's desk because purple is her favorite color. He draws the purple rectangle inside square D2 on the grid.

Gabriella and Manuel both like to draw.
They can draw cool pictures all by themselves!

A
B
C
D
1
2
3
4
Key
= Manuel's desk
= Mrs. Harris's desk
= Gabriella's desk

Manuel's favorite part of his classroom is the story rug. This is where Mrs. Harris reads to the class. Manuel and his friends can sit there when they read by themselves. The story rug is a red circle, so Manuel draws a red circle on his grid. He draws it in square B4 because it's in the back of the classroom.

Manuel likes the story rug because he loves to read!

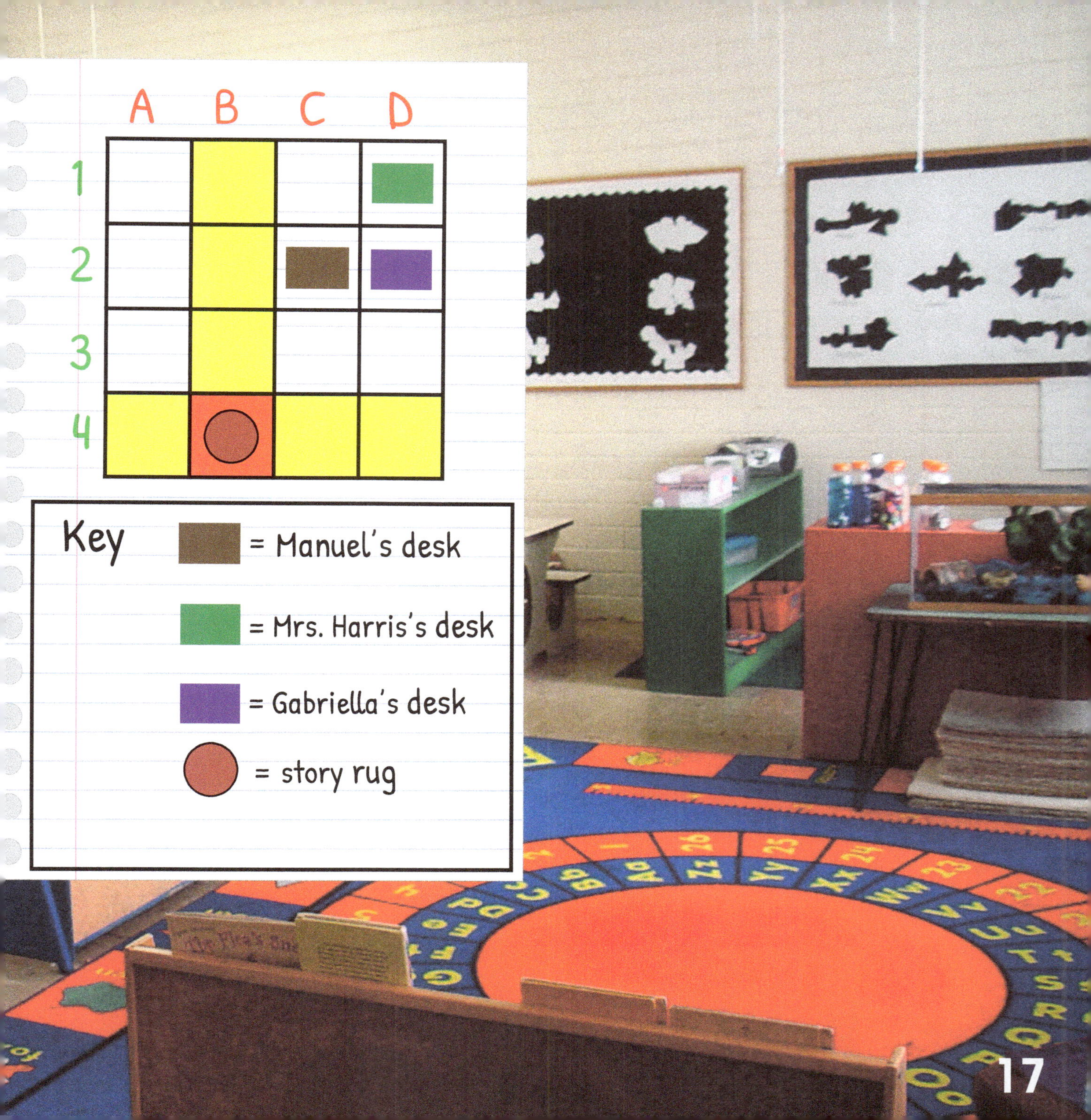
A B C D
1
2
3
4
Key
= Manuel's desk
= Mrs. Harris's desk
= Gabriella's desk
= story rug

Can You Find It?

Manuel is almost done making his classroom map! The last things he adds are the three windows in his classroom. He uses a blue rectangle as the symbol for each window because he can see the blue sky through the windows. Can you find the windows on Manuel's grid?

Can you name the squares on the grid that show where the windows are all by yourself?

A B C D
1
2
3
4
Key
= Manuel's desk
= Mrs. Harris's desk
= Gabriella's desk
= story rug
= window

A Special Map

Manuel is very proud of the map he made all by himself. He takes it home and shows it to his grandma. She can use it to see for herself where things are in Manuel's classroom. Now that Manuel can make grids, he loves learning about maps even more. He can't wait to make more maps!

Manuel's grandma is very proud of him. She's going to hang up his map in the kitchen so everyone can see his classroom!

Make Your Own Map!

It's easy to make a grid just like Manuel's! All you have to do is follow these steps.

Make a big square.

↓

Use lines to make little squares inside the big square.

↓

Write letters across the top.

↓

Write numbers down the side.

↓

Make a key using symbols for things on the map.

↓

Draw the symbols in the squares on the grid.

Glossary

column (KAH-luhm) A line of things that go up and down.

globe (GLOHB) A map of the world shaped like a ball.

horizontal (hohr-uh-ZAHN-tuhl) Going from side to side.

symbol (SIHM-buhl) Something that stands for something else.

vertical (VUHR-tih-kuhl) Going up and down.

Index